VOLUNTEERS

WITHDRAWN

SAGE HUMAN SERVICES GUIDES, VOLUME 5

SAGE HUMAN SERVICES GUIDES

*a series of books edited by ARMAND LAUFFER and published in coopera-
tion with the Continuing Education Program in the Human Services of the
University of Michigan School of Social Work.*

VOLUNTEERS

Armand LAUFFER
Sarah GORODEZKY

with contributions by
Jay Callahan and **Carla Overberger**

Published in cooperation with the Continuing Education Program in the Human Services of the University of Michigan School of Social Work

SAGE PUBLICATIONS   Beverly Hills   London

For information address:

SAGE Publications, Inc.
275 South Beverly Drive
Beverly Hills, California 90212

SAGE Publications Ltd
28 Banner Street
London EC1Y 8QE

Printed in the United States of America

Library of Congress Cataloging in Publication Data

Lauffer, Armand
    Volunteers.

    (Sage human services guides ; v. 5)
    Bibliography: p. 75
    1. Volunteer workers in social services—Handbooks, manuals, etc. I. Gorodezky, Sarah, joint author.
II. Title.
HV41.L323   658.3'7'36102   77-9003
ISBN 0-8039-0884-9

CONTENTS

VOLUNTEERS is one of the series of *Sage Human Services Guides* distributed by Sage Publications in cooperation with the Continuing Education Program in the Human Services of the University of Michigan School of Social Work. Professor Armand Lauffer is Series Editor.

This document was developed in part through two grants. A 1973 grant from the State of Michigan, Office of Substance Abuse Services permitted development of an earlier draft. Beth Reed was Project Director. A 1976 grant by the Edna McConnell Clark Foundation permitted refining and testing of the document through Project CRAFT. Armand Lauffer is Project Director. Earlier versions were tested with populations concerned with alcoholism and drug abuse, and with adoption and foster care. The current document is written in generic terms to be useful in a variety of human service settings.

INTRODUCTION

Many social agencies and other providers of human services expand or extend their services through the work of volunteers. Some organizations would not be in business at all without them. In your organization you may find this handbook useful if you are:

- an agency director, planner, supervisor;
- a volunteer coordinator, especially if you are new to the job;
- considering implementing or expanding a volunteer program in your agency or improving an existing volunteer program;
- an agency administrator or supervisor interested in expanding community input to your program(s), or extending your programs to the community.

We have organized this handbook around the tasks performed in the operation of volunteer programs in human service agencies—those that offer social, educational, health and mental health, protective, counseling and related services. These tasks include program design; recruitment and selection; orientation and training; supervision; working with boards and lay committees; and working with the volunteers as advocates for the agency and for clients. Before we examine these tasks, it may be useful to ask a basic question. Why use volunteers in the first place?

Although this may seem like a logical starting point in evaluating an existing agency volunteer program or in designing a new one, the answers may be more complex than they seem. Some agency personnel just begin with the assumption "the more staff (volunteer or paid), the better." Others want little to do with volunteers. Still others think that it's a good idea to have volunteers but have no idea of how to assign them responsibilities.

Although we will deal with the question "why?," we won't be able to give you all the answers that fit your agency or work situation. Nor do we recommend that all agencies utilize volunteers. In some settings, volunteer programs just do not seem to work. The costs some'times outweigh the benefits. The tasks assigned to volunteers may be inappropriate. In many cases, however, past efforts to use volunteers may have been unsuccessful because not enough attention was paid to the operational requirements for a successful program.

To help you avoid some of the mistakes made by others, this handbook will examine:

— the pros and cons of working with volunteers;

— the tasks involved in initiating and operating a volunteer program; and

— the problems in managing those tasks as they relate to your own agency.

Chapter 1

WHY VOLUNTEERS?

If you have volunteers working in or on behalf of your organization, or are contemplating utilizing volunteers, chances are they will be involved in one or more of the following sets of activities:

– providing direct service to clients;

– performing clerical or administrative tasks;

– public relations;

– fund raising;

– policy making and advising.

VOLUNTEERS FOR When volunteers provide direct services—
DIRECT SERVICE such as counseling ex-prisoners, driving disabled clients to a health clinic, tutoring children in math, crisis phone counseling—they extend an agency's services and the work of the agency's staff. There are many advantages to using volunteers for providing direct services.

Paid professional staff are freed to perform tasks that are more pressing and more closely aligned with their special expertise. For example, crisis phone and walk-in centers often use volunteers for initial interviewing which enables paid staff to provide in-depth counseling and follow-up. The range of services your agency provides can be extended to new populations. One mental health center uses volunteers to screen pre-school children for possible physical or emotional problems, a service previously not available. The range of services offered by your agency may be expanded beyond the paid staff's interests and skills. Examples include establishing a home visiting program for older home-bound persons and creating a teen theater workshop or music group in a school or community center.

In addition, volunteers often exude a level of enthusiasm and personal commitment that is contagious. This can have a positive effect on both clients and paid staff and lend an image of concern to the agency. Moreover, volunteers sometimes speak the clients' language more directly than paid staff. This is especially true if volunteers are of the same ethnic, racial, or religious group, or are from the same socio-economic population as the clients. Their identification with clients and the agency often makes them strong advocates of both clients' rights and the agency's program.

But there may be costs as well. Training and supervising volunteers may take time away from other duties. It takes a certain degree of commitment to recruit, orient and supervise volunteers. The high turnover rate in many volunteer programs may make the costs higher than the benefits. Services are disrupted when volunteers quit or call in saying that other commitments may make it impossible for them to come in during their scheduled time.

A related problem is found in the variable levels of competence among volunteers. Since most volunteers will probably not have gone through a professional training program, you can't assume that they will have comparable levels of competence. While some volunteers may be highly skilled and others learn quickly, some just won't develop the way you might hope they would. Their personal expectations of themselves may be higher than is realistic. They may not be satisfied unless they assume responsibilities that they consider to be "professional". They may not want to undertake tasks they consider mundane or routine.

Volunteers, after all, need rewards like everyone else. And if the rewards don't come from pay and promotion, they must come out of the experiences and relationships volunteers develop working with staff, with each other and with clients. For the most part, satisfaction must be intrinsic to the work situation—a situation that requires at least some attention by the professional staff.

Some professional or paid staff may not like having volunteers around. It may be hard for them to work with others who don't share a common background. It may be even more difficult to give up a cherished task that one has considered "professional" or the prerogative of paid staff. There are some other problems too. By expanding the number of people serving clients, your agency may also risk a breach of client confidentiality. Clients and their records may become more accessible than they were. Potential carelessness with confidential information may cause damage both to the client and to the agency. Finally, some clients just won't talk to a volunteer. "Sally's too much like us," complained a resident of a low income neighborhood about a volunteer in a mental health clinic. "I come here to talk to a professional. I can talk to Sally anytime in the (housing) project. Besides I don't want her knowing any more about my problems than she already knows."

Before deciding to develop or expand a direct service volunteer program in your agency, you'll have to consider the potential payoffs or benefits, and the probable costs. Why not make up your own inventory? Think in terms of the pros and cons for the managers or supervisors in your agency, for the staff who will work with or be affected by the direct services of the volunteers, and for the clients.

Use the form on page 12. Fill in all the pros and cons you can think of. Make up your own version or duplicate this form if you need additional copies. Identify all the pros and cons for management, for the direct service staff in your agency, and for your clients. Use shorthand words such as "more personal," "frees up time," "reduces confidentiality." Are there more pros than cons? Do the pros outnumber the cons? What about the weights? Are the benefits of sufficient weight to balance the costs, even if the number of pros is higher than the number of cons?

CLERICAL   So much, for the moment, for volunteers who
VOLUNTEERS   might provide direct services to clients and
             groups. What about the other categories of
volunteers? Those who perform clerical or administrative tasks may be engaged in typing and filing, serving as receptionists or making appointments, answering the telephone, mailing out books or brochures on request, cataloging, and similar tasks. Many of the

Exercise 1

A BALANCE SHEET OF THE PROS AND CONS OF USING VOLUNTEERS TO TO PROVIDE DIRECT SERVICES TO CLIENTS

	For Management	For Direct Service Staff	For Clients
C O N S			
P R O S			

considerations regarding pros and cons apply here as well. These volunteers reduce the demand on paid staff time and expand the range of tasks performed. But, they also require special handling, administrative time, and so on. The issue of client confidentiality may be as crucial here as with direct service volunteers.

PUBLIC RELATIONS AND FUNDING We also spoke of volunteers who engage in public relations and fund-raising activities. Rather than providing direct services or supportive clerical services, these persons extend the capacities of management and of the agency's planning staff. PR efforts may include: writing publicity or news releases or editing a newsletter for the agency; public speaking; and face-to-face interpretation of the agency's activities or missions. For example, a parent might invite other parents home for coffee and discuss the program of the summer camp. An ex-offender might talk to high school kids about drug abuse and what the drug clinic can do for them if they get into trouble. Some of these tasks go beyond PR, serving an outreach or client recruitment function.

There are also a number of potential costs in using volunteers in this way. The volunteers may not fully appreciate what the agency can do or is willing to do. Volunteers may have their own agendas and may not be able to differentiate them from those of the agency for which they are presumable speaking.

For many voluntary agencies, fund raising is central to survival. Without volunteers to plan and organize a fund-raising campaign and to provide the thousands of hours required to mount successful door-to-door, telephone or mail campaigns, an agency might not be able to continue providing its services. Paid staff, if required to do fund raising, would be diverted from the tasks for which they were hired and trained. Paid staff involvement in fund raising could be viewed as self-serving and might not be sufficiently effective.

Grantsmanship is another approach to fund raising. Seeking contract or grant possibilities, negotiating with potential funding sources and preparing acceptable proposals require special skills. These are often in short supply in those agencies that are primarily involved in the provision of direct services. Sophisticated and committed volunteers can offer much in this area. Again, however, there may be costs to pay. Those who have access to funds or have access to those who control needed funds, can exert considerable influence on the agency. In some ways, their influence may be similar to those who serve on the agency's boards or advisory committees.

POLICY MAKING   A different set of considerations applies
AND ADVISING   when involving volunteers as policy makers
                     or program advisors. There are volunteers
you may wish to involve in ad hoc structures. Volunteers on a transportation task force for the elderly, for example, may be charged with responsibility to lay out a range of alternatives for consideration by the district transportation authority. We find another example in the members of a planning group that helps you select appropriate content for a training program.

Volunteers may be recruited for more regular and ongoing functions, such as participation in the advisory council for a multi-county drug abuse program, or on the board of directors of the family service agency, or in the local council on aging. Members of these policy and advisory groups often include a mix of professionally trained persons, persons who have an interest in or commitment to the issues being addressed and who may represent the influentials in the community, and representatives of the populations or client groups that are likely to be mostly directly affected by the policies and resultant services and programs provided by your agency.

In such cases, volunteers bring prestige and legitimacy to the agency. Legitimacy is the elusive element that an agency needs if it is to have access to the clients it wishes to serve and to the resources it needs to serve them—such as money, facilities, or personnel. When clients, funders, community influentials, and other service providers agree with the agency's definition of its mission or the agency's right to serve specific populations in certain ways, the agency has legitimacy.

Legitimacy can be conferred on your agency by involving others who are legitimate in the eyes of their constituencies and whose presence on your board or advisory committee confers legitimacy on you. Prestige is a similar quality. It refers to the power to command admiration of others and may enhance an organization's legitimacy. That's why task forces to plan new services often have on them volunteers who are representatives of other legitimate service providers and why new agencies often recruit representatives of the population they wish to serve for their boards of directors.

Volunteers engaged in policy making and advising can serve in other areas as well. They may act as a buffer between your agency and others in the community. This is especially true when the agency is under public criticism or when community people turn the "heat" on the staff, demanding a new service. Standing between the staff and various pressure groups, volunteers may be effective in reducing or deflecting external pressures.

On the more positive side, they can add to the brainpower of the staff, contributing new ideas and reflecting the interests of various groups in the community. In effect, they may serve as a bridge between your agency and others in the community, allowing for two-way communications.

There are costs, however. You can't very well ask for advice on something if you don't plan to use the advice you get. Two-way communication may open up the channels for external groups and individuals to put pressure on the agency. If their work is improperly structured or if given tasks beyond their capacities, volunteers on boards and advisory committees may require constant help from the staff, or may come up with ideas that are counter-productive. Once made, their suggestions or decisions are not easy to dismiss.

Having considered all this, it is now your turn again to examine the pros and cons of using volunteers to perform clerical, public relations, fund raising or policy making and advisory tasks. Make up a sheet similar to that used for Exercise 1 or duplicate it with some changed headings. Now list the pros and cons for each of the sets of tasks discussed above. These include conferring prestige and legitimacy on the agency and its services; providing a bridge to its constituencies; buffering criticism; and enlarging the pool of ideas.

As you weigh the pros and cons for the various tasks that volunteers might perform in your agency, you may decide that having them perform direct services is inappropriate, but that expanding the capacity of your paid clerical staff or organizing a PR campaign makes lots of sense. Even if you find that volunteers would be useful in all categories, it may be wise to begin working with them in just a few important tasks. You can always expand the number and types of tasks later.

The conclusions you reach by completing the pros and cons exercise for each category of volunteers can help you focus on those activities that probably will be of most benefit to your agency or on those that will have the best chance of success.

Review the pros and cons sheets you have developed. Now think of how these pros and cons will be evaluated subjectively by influential persons on your agency's paid staff—the people who can make things go or who can stop them from happening. In a recent effort of our own to find out how agency staff might react to expanding a volunteer program, we got the following responses.

Favorable Remarks	Unfavorable Remarks
— "Volunteers are fun to train and work with.	— "It's not easy to manage or to control volunteers."
— "I can get to more clients by working through volunteers."	— "I don't want to give up personal contact with my clients."
— "I like supervising and managing a staff. Volunteers give me a chance to do that."	— "What if they are just as competent as I am?"
— "Mayber they will make my job easier."	— "I don't feel competent enough to be a supervisor."
— "Working with high status volunteers expands my own status and that of the agency."	— "They might be more accepted by the clients than I am."

Do any of these strike a bell? Would similar responses cause you to reconsider the pros and cons you have recorded? Go over the exercise you just completed with the influential staff at your agency. Get them involved early in thinking through costs and benefits. You'll need their input if you expect to design an effective volunteer program.

Chapter 2

DESIGNING A VOLUNTEER PROGRAM

Once you have decided what it is you want the agency's volunteers to do, you'll have to consider how many volunteers will be needed and when. To what departments or work units should they be assigned? How is their work to be supervised and coordinated? Are the agency's current facilities adequate? If you think through each of these issues in a planned way, chances are that volunteers, paid staff, and agency clients will all find the volunteer program more satisfactory than if it is purely ad hoc in its organization and development.

VOLUNTEERS AND PAID STAFF   One of the first programmatic issues you'll have to consider is the relationship between the efforts of volunteers and those of paid staff. Volunteers can extend the work of paid staff by supplementing paid staff activities, such as increasing the number of persons available to answer calls on a drug agency's "hot line." They might further extend the work of paid staff by substituting for paid staff when the latter are unavailable because of more pressing assignments. For example, volunteers may bring low income children to a health screening clinic, permitting the caseworker to spend more time on case findings. Volunteers may also make it possible for an agency to engage in new activities that would otherwise not be undertaken. A fund raising effort might not be possible without the work of volunteers who plan it and conduct it. Similarly, a new "home repair" service might be dependent entirely on volunteers for staffing and coordination.

On the following page, you will find a second exercise. Notice that it includes ten boxes formed by five rows and two columns. The rows represent each of the five major categories of tasks given to volunteers: performing direct services; doing clerical and administrative work; public relations; fund raising; or policy making and advising. The boxes in the left hand column are to be filled in with those volunteer activities that extend the work currently being performed by paid staff by supplementing it or substituting for it. The right hand column is for those activities that would not be conducted without volunteer staff.

Complete the exercise by giving one or two examples of tasks volunteers could perform in each task group under each column. Limit yourself only to those task groups you have decided are appropriate for your agency. You may find this exercise very helpful in deciding how to organize your volunteer program. In general, two possibilities exist.

INTEGRATED   Volunteer activities can be integrated fully
OR SEPARATED   into the ongoing structure of the agency. Clerical volunteers, for example, may be attached to an office staff, performing activities which extend the paid staff's capacities. Direct service volunteers may work directly under the supervision of caseworkers, child guidance counselors, recreation workers, or teachers. In these examples, volunteers are fully integrated into the agency's ongoing operations. While the agency may have an overall volunteer coordinator or supervisor, on a day-to-day basis the individual volunteer's efforts are supervised or directed by a member of the paid staff. In the end, it is the paid staff person who is held accountable for his or her own work, whether performed personally or by the volunteer who extends that staff person's capacities.

In many human service agencies, however, some activities and even some entire service programs may be assigned only to volunteers. In a local museum, for example, a pre-school art program may be conducted entirely by volunteers. The home repair and friendly visiting program of a family service agency may be conducted by volunteers and coordinated by a volunteer who works directly under the director of the agency or in cooperation with the casework supervisor. In these examples, a major agency service

Exercise 2

EXAMPLES OF VOLUNTEER ACTIVITIES

MAJOR TASK GROUP	ACTIVITIES THAT EXTEND THE WORK OF PAID STAFF	ACTIVITIES THAT WOULD NOT BE CONDUCTED WITHOUT VOLUNTEER STAFF
Direct Services		
Clerical		
Public Relations		
Fund Raising		
Policy Making and Advising		

would be non-existent if it were not for volunteers. The same might be true of a neighborhood fund-raising effort, the printing of a weekly newsletter, or the maintenance of an information service. Each of these activities may be entirely dependent on the work of volunteers.

When the volunteer program makes up a separate unit in the organization, you have to take different things into account than when the work volunteers do is integrated into the paid staff's responsibilities. In the latter case, the large amount of interaction and day-to-day independence of paid and volunteer staff requires that lines of authority and areas of responsibility be clearly speci- fied. This is so even when volunteers with similar or greater expertise than the paid staff work almost totally independently. The general pattern is for the volunteer to be supervised by a paid staff person. Some of the tensions which may develop in such relationships are discussed in Chapter 1.

These tensions are often reduced when volunteers perform totally separate services within the agency and are organized into totally volunteer work units. There is, however, a danger that these services may not be considered central to the agency, that they will be misused by paid staff, or that they may be dropped when volunteers are no longer available or interested in providing them. There is also some danger that these programs will be poorly organized because they are dependent on a variable supply of volunteers with given interests and skills. The problems of both integrated and separated volunteer programs can be reduced by careful designation of "work units" and "units of work."

UNITS   A unit of work refers to the cluster of tasks per-
OF WORK   formed by a staff member (paid or volunteer). It
                      can be time-limited (getting a mailing out twice a year), one-time only (leading a workshop for community leaders), or ongoing (doing intake in a rehabilitation agency). Several units of work may be combined in designing a person's job. Most paid staff persons are generally assigned a combination of ongoing, time-limited or one-time only units of work. This is not always so with volunteers whose assignments may be limited to a single unit of work. By clearly defining each unit of work, it is often possible to reduce the tensions between paid and unpaid staff in fully

integrated volunteer programs and to guarantee consistency in separated programs.

In designing a unit of work, consider the activity to be performed. What composes the activity? What is it intended to accomplish? What methods should be used? Who is to provide direction or supervision? To what extent will the volunteer operate on his or her own? And for how long? The following examples may be helpful in defining a unit of work for your agency's volunteers.

SAMPLE UNITS OF WORK

ELEMENTS IN DEFINING A UNIT OF WORK	EXAMPLE A	EXAMPLE B
1. The activity to be performed	Friendly visiting to the homebound	Brochure design
2. To accomplish the result of	Keeping older persons interested in the outside world, identifying their other needs. Referral to other helping services as appropriate.	Recruiting other volunteers
3. Using the following methods	Weekly visits on a scheduled basis to assigned homebound persons, and using agency reporting and follow up forms.	Art work and design
4. On the instructions of or under the supervision of	The supervisor of casework services	Final copy has to be approved by agency director
5. With the following range of choice	Conversation can encompass any subject matter. Suggestions for referrals must be discussed with supervisor prior to further action. Written reports must be turned in within two days of visit.	Administrative and volunteer consideration
6. And in the following time frame	Ongoing, weekly, for 10-12 hours	One-time only

Using the same format, define the units of work expected of one or more of the volunteers in your agency. Use the form for Exercise 3 on page 23. Feel free to duplicate additional copies of the form as needed. Once you've identified all the units of work for each category of volunteers, you can put these together into job descriptions. Job descriptions can be tailored to specific volunteers, taking into account their interests and skills. Or, they can be developed in advance. In this case, volunteers will be recruited to fill those positions described and will be trained to perform the required tasks. By designing a unit of work in this way, it becomes possible to delineate those tasks expected of the volunteer and those expected of paid staff. Don't be surprised if this leads to your specifying the units of work for paid staff as well.

Ask those paid staff members who may ultimately be involved in your program to complete Exercise 3 or to work on it with you. Getting your staff involved in the design and planning process may help reduce problems and tensions that may arise at a later time. Staff with a working knowledge of day-to-day operations have valuable insights into the most efficient and effective ways of organizing volunteer activities. Their early participation may be important in identifying the potential pay-offs of using volunteers and the things that paid staff must do to make the project work.

WORK   The work unit refers to the grouping of staff who
UNITS   perform various units of work. This grouping is for the
          purpose of coordination or supervision. A volunteer may be assigned to an all-volunteer work unit or to one composed of both paid and volunteer staff. The work unit may include professional providers of direct services such as social workers and probation officers, a unit supervisor, and supportive clerical and intake staff. When a volunteer is assigned to a work unit that is composed mainly of paid staff, his or her units of work and their relationships to the units of work performed by other staff must be clearly defined. When a volunteer is assigned to a work unit that is primarily or entirely made up of volunteers, the relationship of that unit to other work units must be clearly defined.

This definition of relationships is sometimes accomplished through development of an organizational chart or a job chart within a particular work unit. Both organizational and job charts can be used to depict the formal relationships between staff

Exercise 3

DEFINING A UNIT OF WORK

ELEMENTS IN DEFINING A UNIT OF WORK	TASK: check one ☐ direct services ☐ clerical ☐ PR ☐ fund raising ☐ policy making and advising
1. The activity to be performed	
2. To accomplish the result of	
3. Using the following methods	
4. On the instructions of or under the supervision of	
5. With the following range of choices	
6. And in the following time frame	

members and between work units. The organizational chart generally depicts the lines of communication between work units
and/or persons. It may depict the formal hierarchy of relationships
(i.e., who supervises whom and to whom an individual or work
unit is responsible). A fuller discussion of organizational charts is
found in the handbook on UNDERSTANDING YOUR SOCIAL
AGENCY in this series. The job chart generally depicts who is
responsible for what units of work within a work unit. It can be
used to depict the nature of the relationships between persons in a
work unit. For example, a vertical or pyramidal job chart shows a
hierarchical relationship. A flat or circular chart shows relationships between colleagues. The examples on pages 24 and 25 are
illustrations.

Work units are generally put together around a theme or
"cluster principle." The principle may be the performance of a

JOB CHART FOR A WORK UNIT*

Teen Programs Work Unit

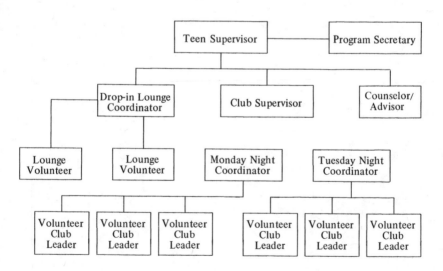

---

*The job chart shows the hierarchial relationships between staff and one work unit. Could
you have broken this chart into three, each depicting a sub work unit? Notice that
volunteers are integrated into a work unit with paid staff. Without them there be much
for the paid staff to do?

ORGANIZATION CHART FOR A COMMUNITY

Board of Directors

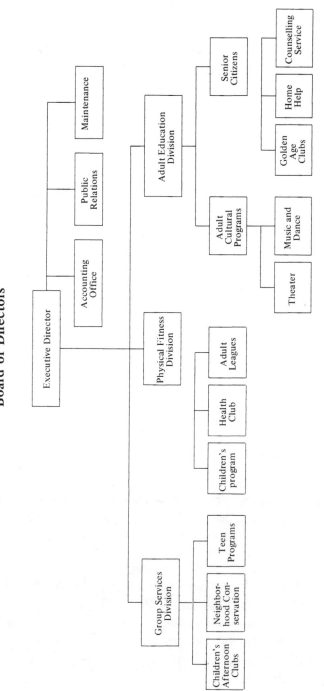

*The organization chart shows the relationship of one work unit to others and indicates where supervision or coordination occur.

particular agency service (e.g., family treatment). It may be geographic, as when staff are assigned to a multi-service unit in a low income neighborhood. It may be aimed at providing services to specific client populations such as pre-school children, members of an ethnic minority, or persons with respiratory diseases. A work unit may also be organized around a "problem area" such as job absenteeism or drug abuse. Finally, some work units provide supportive services such as publicity, a typing or clerical pool, or accounting.

Once you and your staff have made decisions regarding units of work to be performed by volunteers and how volunteers are to be organized in terms of work units, you will be ready to deal with some other program design issues.

NUMBERS, TIME   You will have to determine the optimal
AND TIMING   number of volunteers you want assigned to
                     those tasks selected, the time commitments
you will demand of them, and the amount of paid staff time involved in training, supervision and evaluation.

Remember that volunteers will add to the number of people working in your agency. Additional personnel require additional communication, facilities and time. Do you have enough work space to accommodate extra people? Do current staff assignments allow enough room for supervisory or training responsibilities? Who will be assigned to making sure that there is good communication between volunteers and other agency personnel?

Designating someone to the position of volunteer coordinator is one way of minimizing duplication of efforts, ensuring a clear channel of communication, and providing staff and volunteers with a liaison sensitive to both their needs and the agency's needs. This is especially important if volunteers are to be involved on an ongoing basis and if there is to be more than one work unit. Ordinarily, volunteer coordinators are paid staff whose primary duties involve the administrative aspects of recruitment, selection, orientation, training and evaluation. If you cannot afford to hire someone new for this position or cannot release a paid staff person already in your agency employ, you might consider assigning a volunteer who has administrative experience to this responsibility. If your program is successful, and you can demonstrate its effectiveness and cost efficiency, you may be able to create a salaried position later on.

Be specific on the minimal time commitment you expect from volunteers. The time will vary with the nature of the task. A direct service volunteer in a child guidance clinic may need to commit two or three mornings or afternoons per week to ensure continuity for the clients. A clerical support volunteer may only be needed for five hours per week. Fund raising or public relations may not involve regularly scheduled time commitments.

One final consideration. The timing of the development and expansion of volunteer efforts is central to their success. Volunteer efforts may need phasing-in over time. Success in one work unit may suggest expanding the number of tasks assigned to it or adding new volunteers to that unit or to other work units. After some time, it may lead to the development of new work units, composed entirely or primarily of volunteers performing new services for the agency and its clients.

Chapter 3

RECRUITING VOLUNTEERS

Once you've got a good idea of what it is you want volunteers to do at your agency or on its behalf, you are ready to move to the next step—recruitment. Recruiting requires more than just "putting the word out," tacking up an announcement on a bulletin board, or placing an ad in a newspaper. It requires thinking through the tasks you want performed, the kinds of people you want to perform those tasks, where you might find them, and what the best means of recruitment might be. It also requires making the most effective use of your agency or program's image in recruiting the kind of people you want.

IMAGE   Image refers to the way people view your agency.
    Does it have a highly professional image? Is it perceived to be indigenous to the community? Does serving on the agency's board or on one of its committees confer status on the participant? Is the agency seen as providing important services to its clients? The agency's image will be affected by: (1) the characteristics of its paid staff (their performance, training, personal styles of contacting people in the community, sex, race, cultural background, age); (2) the characteristics of its client population (age, socio-economic characteristics, racial or ethnic identities, representative problems); (3) the agency's resources, such as facilities and level of funding; (4) the kinds of services and other tasks provided by both paid and non-paid staff; and (5) the

effectiveness of the agency's public relations efforts in the community.

To what extent is the agency's image likely to be attractive to the kinds of volunteers you are looking for? To what extent is the image your agency projects a true reflection of what it is? If the paid staff are all highly trained but include few if any representatives of minorities, will the agency be able to attract minority persons who live in a low income neighborhood to perform direct service tasks? Will a drug abuse center staffed by ex-addicts and street people be able to attract prestigious persons to its board?

The image projected by many agencies is at least partially misleading. Thus, perceptions of the agency by prospective volunteers may be totally or partially incorrect. If this is true in your agency's case, what might you do to adjust the erroneous public image? What kind of information should prospective volunteers have about your agency so that they'll know whether or not it is the place for them? You may find Exercise 4 helpful in thinking through this question.

INFORMATION   If you found yourself unsure about how to
GIVING   get information out to people, don't worry.
APPROACHES   We've got some suggestions for you. Look
                over the inventory which follows. Are you
currently using any of these approaches? How well do they work? Which additional ones might work better or might compliment those currently in use?

Whatever approaches you use, they should be aimed directly at those populations from which you want to recruit volunteers or at others who might recruit them for you. Shotgun information campaigns might do a lot for your agency's image, but they are costly in terms of time and effort and don't always produce results as good as those coming from more targeted efforts.

The following inventory may give you some ideas on how to pitch your information to specific populations.

(1) Insert advertisements in local, ethnic and "underground" newspapers as appropriate. A local merchant might pay for the ad in return for a small thanks at the bottom. Consider also organizational newsletters as good sources of "free" advertising that reach large numbers of people.

Exercise 4

INFORMATION NEEDED BY PROSPECTIVE VOLUNTEERS

1. Category of volunteer: [ ]   direct service
                                 [ ]   clerical
                                 [ ]   fund raising
                                 [ ]   public relations
                                 [ ]   policy making and advising

2. What information does the potential volunteer need about the agency?

_____

_____

_____

_____

3. Is this information currently available? From whom? To whom?

_____

_____

4. If it is not sufficiently available or accurate, how could you get the correct information to prospective volunteers?

_____

_____

_____

5. Are you currently using any formal or informal means of getting out information on your agency or its program that might be redirected to prospective volunteers?

_____

_____

_____

6. What other considerations should go into your information strategy?

_____

_____

_____

(2) Display fliers and posters in schools, stores, laundromats, and banks. Consider bulletin boards of such places as a planned parenthood office, women's centers, recreation agencies, and other well-traveled community spots. But don't just put up the information because people will see it. Think about which groups you are recruiting in deciding where fliers should be distributed or displayed.

Fliers can be designed as handouts that describe a particular problem or the needs of a specific population such as the elderly home-bound. A flier might indicate how volunteers provide services to the home-bound. Handouts might also list the skills required such as typing, driving or interviewing.

Fliers and posters should be attractively and neatly done. Consider recruiting a volunteer with some advertising and art skills if no one on the paid staff has these skills.

(3) News stories in the local press can be a good source of free publicity for volunteer recruitment. They can also do a good deal for the agency's image. Most papers have "human interest" or "people" sections. Find out who the editors of these sections are for your local papers. Establish personal contacts. Let the editors know what your agency is doing in areas that may be newsworthy. The roles of volunteers in these endeavors can be described in articles. Make sure articles include a contact person and phone number for persons interested in volunteering.

Many papers also have "involvement" or "volunteer opportunity" columns. These are usually short paragraphs highlighting the types of volunteer tasks available and contact persons and phone numbers of the agencies involved.

(4) Writing letters to the editor of local newspapers can be very effective in recruitment, especially when written by experienced volunteers or knowledgeable community citizens. These letters can also be used to give recognition to volunteers themselves, if written by agency administrators or board officers thanking a particular group for services rendered. This could serve to provide incentive for already active volunteers and function as a recruitment strategy as well.

(5) Get spot announcements on radio, commercial and publicly sponsored television. All broadcasting stations are required to air a specified number of public service announcements at regular intervals. Local stations prefer to use local "spots." Consider producing a short video tape on some aspect of your agency or program. Does anyone connected with your agency have film-making skills?

(6) Arrange speaking engagements for paid and volunteer staff and board members at educational and community based organizations. These might include churches, clubs, civic groups, and schools.

(7) Word of mouth by the volunteers already on the job is also a very effective recruiting tool. Obviously, this type of recruitment can only be used when your volunteer program has been underway for a time and has produced a core of active volunteers.

We are certain you have other ideas and experiences of your own. In Exercise 5, fill in the spaces with information on the populations for which you might want to use the recruitment method on the left. Consider the category of volunteers you are recruiting.

For example, next to	*Clerical volunteer from*
Advertisements you	*the Northside School*
might list:	*District*

Creative PR need not be expensive. An agency we know of in a northern state used the marquee of the local drive-in all winter. An agency serving college students received free publicity from a campus bookstore which printed relevant information on a bookmark given away with each sale.

REFERRALS   Think also of getting "referrals." Just as your agency gets client referrals, it should be able to get volunteer referrals. The following are some fairly common sources of referrals.

— Other social agencies and human service organizations, especially those with agency volunteer programs. If you have a local Volunteer Action Center, maintain regular contact with it. Exchange skilled volunteers among agencies providing coordinated services in the community.

— Former volunteers. A carefully selected group of former volunteers can be recruited to share their experience and access to the community.

— Community organizations such as Kiwanis, Jaycees, PTA, Lion's Club, artistic, musical, professional and senior citizens groups. These may be both a direct source of volunteers and a source of referrals.

— Students from local high schools, colleges, and community colleges. They may need to undertake internships and practicums in agencies to fill curriculum requirements. The school may require that someone be available to supervise and provide feedback to the students and the

Exercise 5

INVENTORY OF APPROACHES FOR GETTING THE INFORMATION OUT	POPULATION FOR WHICH THE APPROACH MAKES SENSE
1. *Advertisements*	1. _____
2. *Fliers and Posters*	2. _____
3. *News Stories*	3. _____
4. *Letters to the Editor*	4. _____
5. *Spot Announcements*	5. _____
6. *Speaking Engagements*	6. _____
7. *Word of Mouth*	7. _____
8.	8. _____

school. Be sure that such a person is available before you approach the school and remember that student placement periods are often very short and the help you get may not compensate for the time you'll have to put into orientation, training and supervision. On the other hand, a student may stay beyond the placement. One community center, for example, regularly recruits its summer volunteers from among the students placed in the agency during the school year.

HANDOUTS When making a contact with another agency or organization, try to be as informative and personal as you can. If you want others to join your agency, you will want to present your agency's image in the best possible terms. Be positive in your approach, but also be realistic. Do not oversell the rewards or underplay the difficulties. Some agencies have found that having written materials available can be very helpful in recruiting. The sample on page 36 may give you some ideas on how to pattern your own handout material.

Keep your handouts general enough so you do not discourage people from applying. List several skill areas or attributes you are seeking, as in the sample recruitment handout on page 36. On the other hand, it is a waste of time and effort to recruit people who are obviously not appropriate for the job. A properly designed handout might help prospective volunteers screen themselves in or out before they contact your agency. By specifying information such as age requirements, if any, length of commitment required, and so on, you can reduce wasted time as well as potential misunderstandings.

Some agencies use more than a single handout. While an extensive packet of materials may be more than you need, we thought it might be helpful to examine what one mental health center put together in a packet used to brief its experienced volunteers and board members on how to recruit volunteers. It includes:

— A brochure that describes the agency and includes data on its programs and services, its history and its funding sources.

— A list of key staff members and their responsibilities plus the names of board members and committee chairpersons.

— Sample program announcements describing specific services and special events offered in previous years.

SAMPLE RECRUITMENT HANDOUT

LOOKING FOR AN OUTLET FOR YOUR BRAINS AND COMPASSION?

We've got one for you at Crossroads Center.

IF YOU

- want to help staff design new services for older people;
- like to visit with people and are good at cheering them up;
- have a car and don't mind chauffeuring people who can't get around without some help; or
- have clerical skills.

WE NEED YOU FOR

- planning and committee work
- five to ten hours of driving per week (we furnish the gas and the liability insurance)
- office work between two and five mornings per week
- counseling and friendly visits two or more mornings per week.

WE CAN'T OFFER YOU PAY, BUT WE CAN OFFER YOU

- training and orientation when you first get started
- the satisfaction of working with other dedicated volunteers
- a chance to learn about and contribute to your community
- the knowledge that what you're doing for others really counts

INTERESTED? CALL
Marilyn Schwartz
Volunteer Coordinator
CROSSROADS CENTER
Abel at Baker
Charlestown, 40892 (719) 665-7651

Volunteer
Characteristics

Tasks

Rewards

Whom to
Contact

— A calendar of coming events listing all community and family education activities scheduled.

— Samples of newsletters and reports.

— An answer sheet on most frequently asked questions about the agency, the same sheet used by staff in a recent community meeting aimed at interpreting the agency to potential clients.

VOLUNTEERS'   An information campaign that focuses only
NEEDS AND   on the agency and its needs may not be
INTERESTS   effective. Volunteers may not get paid, but
they don't work for nothing. They have interests and needs of their own. In our experience, we've found that people are motivated to offer their services on a voluntary basis when volunteer activities provide:

— an outlet for doing good or helping those less fortunate;

— an opportunity to learn, to develop new skills, or to build a background of experience that might lead to other work;

— social satisfactions, stemming from interaction with other volunteers, with staff and with clients; or

— expression of one's social or religious commitments.

The intrinsic rewards that speak to these motivations may be insufficient without some other more concrete incentives. These include:

— Opportunities to attend in-service and staff development programs with paid staff.

— Structured career ladder opportunities for more responsible and experienced volunteers, such as supervision of new volunteers, assignments of more difficult cases, increased administrative roles, and the like. These types of opportunities, based on the interests of the persons involved, can be positive incentives for volunteers to remain active and motivated.

— Letters of recommendation for future employment or educational endeavors.

— Reimbursement for out-of-pocket expenses such as travel, parking and babysitting.

— Insurance coverage while on the job. It is now possible, at a low cost, for an agency to insure its volunteers against work-connected injury. More detailed information about this insurance can be found in Appendix B.

— A luncheon or dinner at which staff thank volunteers for their efforts. This can take the form of a formal awards or recognition banquet or it can be an informal get-together in which volunteers are "treated" at a favorite eating spot. A relatively small and inexpensive gesture such as this can be very gratifying to volunteers.

Be careful not to demand or expect too much. Remember that most volunteers:

— have other commitments and may be limited in time and energy;

— may be unaware of their own abilities to do the job and may need support through training and supervision;

— want to be sure that what they are getting into will be rewarding; and

— are just as anxious as others to be liked and appreciated.

Volunteers will be willing to undertake tasks for which they receive no pay, some of which may be dull or unpleasant, but only if their own needs and interests are at least partially met.

You'll have a better idea of how to pitch your recruitment efforts once you have thought through the qualities you are looking for in your agency's volunteers. These are discussed in Chapter 4.

Chapter 4

SCREENING AND SELECTING POTENTIAL VOLUNTEERS

Some agencies are in such need of additional help, they seem unable to turn away anyone who volunteers his or her services. Other agencies employ a highly selective process of screening potential volunteers. Generally some form of screening is essential if you are to select the right volunteers and if they are to get into the right jobs. Screening refers to a procedure whereby the agency determines whether or not a prospective volunteer fits a job or work assignment, and gives the prospective volunteer a chance to check him or herself out against the demands of the job. It gives both the agency and the volunteer a chance to get to know each other before deciding on a match.

WHO TO   A screening process must be carefully designed and *SCREEN*   consistently managed. It takes staff time and energy.

And it requires knowing what kinds of volunteers you want for different jobs. To what extent should a volunteer's background or experience be similar to that of the agency's paid staff? To what extent should the volunteers have similar life experiences to those of the agency's clientele?

Some agencies employ previous clients in helping roles under the assumption that one who has coped with a problem can bring a special understanding to working with others with a similar problem. Other agencies claim that "recovered" clients are unable to be objective in permitting an individual to find his or her own solution to a problem. It is not uncommon for people actually

needing service to approach an agency with an offer to volunteer.
It is important to be alert to those needing help who come to the
agency in the guise of wanting to provide help.

The referral services discussed in Chapter 3 sometimes are used
to "pre-screen" volunteers. Other social agencies, for example,
might spot someone who could fit perfectly into your volunteer
program. Former or current volunteers might be asked to screen
potential volunteers, checking them out while also giving the
potential volunteer a chance to check out the agency. Schools can
be asked to pre-screen students who might be interested in the
agency.

The kinds of persons sought will depend on the positions for
which they are sought. One kind of screening process might be
required for persons who may be appointed to policy and advisory
committees. A nominating committee made up of volunteers
might do the screening. Staff, on the other hand, might do the
screening of direct service volunteers. The job may be assigned to
either paid or volunteer staff in the service or clerical work units
involved, or to an agency volunteer coordinator—a person assigned
to manage all or most volunteer efforts. The executive director, or
his or her designate, on the other hand, might screen and select
volunteers to be involved in fund raising and public relations.

REGULATIONS   In many situations, the agency determines
                    what kinds of volunteers it wants for which
positions. But in some areas, state agencies or professional
associations regulate the use of direct service volunteers. Rules and
regulations may stipulate conditional behavior of all employees of
a program or may single out volunteers as a specific group. If such
regulations exist in your state, find out what they are.

TIMING   While many agencies screen potential volunteers right
               at the start, others prefer to delay the screening
process until the completion of a volunteer training or orientation
program. Several "timing" possibilities exist.

– Screen first, train later.

– Train first, screen later.

– Train, without screening, letting people screen themselves in or out.

– Pre-screen, train, then re-screen.

The order you choose may depend upon available staff time; the difficulty of the tasks assigned to volunteer workers; the possibility that volunteer error could lead to serious consequences for the agency and its clients; the categories of volunteers sought (board members, fund raisers, etc.).

The screen-train-re-screen option will give you the most information about a prospective volunteer. An initial screening procedure will provide you with data on the prospective volunteer's potential for work in your agency. The re-screening after training assures you at least some additional information on which to evaluate whether that potential has become reality. This process also allows you to take a chance on prospective volunteers about whom you are not absolutely certain, and gives them the opportunity to demonstrate their capabilities.

Remember, recruitment, if carefully designed, can serve as a screening process, especially for tasks requiring a specific skill or type of experience or time commitment. This can save your agency time and effort.

SCREENING APPARATUS   Prospective volunteers may be required to fill out application forms before participating in more extensive screening procedures. These forms can be as simple or as detailed as seems appropriate for you and your agency. Be careful about the language of applications if your volunteers are not fluent in English. For some people, filling out an application is itself an insurmountable task.

Consider adopting what one agency volunteer coordinator does to avoid an anxiety reaction to forms. He uses an application form but fills it out himself while asking the questions of the applicant. This is done during an initial interview. Starting with such questions as age, address, phone number, and educational background helps to put the applicant at ease. It is also easier for some people to discuss why they want to volunteer and relevant aspects of their past experiences orally rather than to put such information in written form.

Forms are useful as screening devices. If the applicant is clearly not suitable because of age, background or other characteristics, you can inform the applicant on the spot that initial requirements have not been met. Application forms are also useful in evaluating different aspects of your volunteer program. For example, by asking, "Where did you find out about the program?," you may be able to gather information on which aspects of your publicity campaign seem to be the most effective.

The most common methods of screening prospective direct service volunteers are the use of group processes, psychological tests, and interviews. These techniques may be used separately or together. Combinations of the techniques net you the most information about a person, but will also take the greatest amount of staff time and energy. The most effective method(s) of screening volunteers will provide information about the volunteer's ability to perform the tasks required by the agency. Look at the "handouts" you have already developed for volunteer positions and consider what methods will be most useful and accurate in determining whether a specific volunteer can fill the position. The "job description" you will be developing in Exercise 4 may be even more helpful.

GROUP METHODS   A group interview may be a one-time event or a series of such interviews may be conducted over a period of time. For example, a number of prospective volunteers may meet once a month with a paid and a volunteer staff member. Together they explore the personal strengths, skills, and attitudes needed for effective volunteer service. Both staff and prospective volunteer get to know one another. But group methods are sometimes overrated. It is difficult to generalize accurately from an individual's behavior in the group to the tasks he or she may be required to perform as an individual. If your agency does not have staff members experienced in running groups, the process may be time-consuming and expensive, yielding few returns. This is especially true for a small agency needing only a few volunteers.

PSYCHOLOGICAL   Psychological tests are usually used in
TESTS   combination with other methods. Tests can
                 be used to provide an objective measure of applicant qualifications, and are particularly useful in measuring a volunteer's stability and emotional maturity. But the validity of test results may be questioned. It may be hard to get a test that fits your particular volunteer's job. Moreover, an experienced

tester must be available to administer and interpret results. All this may make the use of tests more trouble than it's worth.

INTERVIEWS   Because arranging staff time for interviews is more manageable and requires skill that is more common than testing or group methods, interviews are the most common and appear to be the preferred method of screening. Yet, interviews place a great deal of importance on a relatively brief encounter. The person who does well in an interview is not necessarily the best person for the job. Nevertheless, since the interview is the most often used screening procedure, a closer look at what makes a good interview may be helpful. Keep the following suggestions in mind when establishing an interview procedure for your volunteer program.

— Carefully choose the staff members who will conduct the interviews. The greater the number of people interviewing, the more likely it is that different standards will be applied to prospective volunteers. If collective decisions are made, interviewers must agree upon standards and desired outcomes.

— Use an interview schedule (or guide) to assure general agreement both among the interviewers themselves and the interviewers and the agency administrators about what information is needed to asses an applicant's qualifications for a position.

— Have job descriptions available, specifying the tasks and time commitments necessary for the job. Is prior training necessary?

— The screening interview is an ideal time to examine the components of a contract, specifying what the volunteer and the agency can expect from one another. A sample volunteer contract is found in Chapter 5.

— Establish a procedure for letting the volunteer know if he or she was accepted or not, and why the decision was made.

REJECTING   The most difficult part of any screening proce-
APPLICANTS   dure is the rejection of a prospective volunteer.
                  The four suggestions which follow may help ease
the situation:

— When you reject someone for a particular position, give explicit reasons for doing so. These should be based upon the needs of your program and the skills you identified as necessary to achieve its goals. Such feedback is most believable if it includes specifics from the interview itself or other screening approaches used.

  – Include some positive statements about the volunteer's behavior or experiences so as to ease the blow.

  – If there are other positions or tasks within the agency for which the applicant is qualified, suggest those as alternatives.

  – Develop a resource list of other agencies that use volunteers to which the applicant might be referred.

Remember, rejection will always involve some discomfort. Your thoughtfulness in providing specific feedback should make the situation more bearable both for you and the applicant. Don't be a "softy" if you are quite certain the applicant is not right for the job. And don't allow yourself to pervert the meaning of volunteerism by thinking, "after all, it's just a volunteer job. Why not give the person a break?" Asking someone to do something you know she or he cannot do is unfair to both the applicant and to your agency.

JOB   The screening process is more accurate if you
DESCRIPTIONS   use job descriptions that list specific tasks and
                    responsibilities expected of the volunteer. For it to be useful, the job description for each volunteer should be as complete as possible. In designing a volunteer job description, build it from other job descriptions for similar work at your agency or other agencies. If these do not exist, you have to start from scratch.

Begin by identifying the units of work to be performed. Consider what the volunteer is to do, how she or he is to do it, why, and the level of skill involved. The example on page 45 comes from an information and referral service for the aging.

Although much of the preceding discussion focused on the volunteer who provides a direct service, it can be generalized to those doing clerical work, PR and fund raising for an agency. The conditions for volunteers performing advisory and policy making tasks are a bit different and are dealt with more explicitly in Chapter 6 of this handbook.

Using Exercise 6 to guide you, draw up a job description for a volunteer or category of volunteers. Consider the following.

  – How are the clients to be assigned to volunteers or paid staff?

  – Are both expected to do similar work, fill out similar forms?

SAMPLE: VOLUNTEER JOB DESCRIPTION

1. Title of job: "Friendly visitor"

2. Supervised by: assigned agency caseworker

3. Duties & Responsibilities (the what and the how of the job unit):
   - telephone assigned, older home-bound persons to arrange appointments;
   - visit home-bound persons weekly to talk to them and to identify any special problems they have with which the agency can help;
   - identify other potential clients for the agency;
   - complete an agency form reporting what is discussed and any problems identified during the visit; and
   - agree to work at least five hours weekly.

4. Qualifications:
   - ability to relate to and to elicit responses from others;
   - sympathy for the aged and aging; and
   - knowledge of the ethnic and/or socio-economic groups that the agency's home-bound clients represent.

5. Purpose of job:
   - to keep home-bound connected with the community;
   - to reduce home-bound individuals' sense of isolation;
   - to identify problems that call for agency intervention; and
   - to give volunteers meaningful, important work.

— Do paid staff supervise the volunteers doing similar work?

A well designed job description not only gives the agency staff person a guide for screening, but helps volunteers screen themselves in or out. But self-screening is not always accurate. The most accurate job descriptions specify the units of work to be performed. But it is not always possible to do this. It is sometimes better not to be too specific, especially when you want to tailor a job to the interests and capacities of a talented or committed volunteer.

Nevertheless, job descriptions that are written in overly general terms are easily misinterpreted by outsiders. You may have to do some interpreting during the individual or group interview. If a volunteer does not quite fit the needs implied in the job description, you may be able to bend the job to fit the volunteer, especially if the volunteer possesses characteristics you consider important to your program. Screening, then, means not only finding the person to fit the job, but it may also require finding the job to fit the person.

Exercise 6

DESIGNING A VOLUNTEER JOB DESCRIPTION

1. Title of Job: _____

2. Supervised by: _____

   _____

3. Duties and _____
   Responsibilities
   (the *what* and the _____
   how of the job _____
   units; include
   hours needed): _____

   _____

4. Qualifications (including training, _____
   experience, background, etc.): _____

   _____

   _____

   _____

5. Location (address, phone _____
   number, office location,
   and relationship to other _____
   departments if appro-
   priate): _____

   _____

NOW STOP AND THINK FOR A MOMENT! DOES THIS JOB DESCRIPTION MATCH THE HANDOUT YOU ARE USING TO RECRUIT VOLUNTEERS? MAKE ADJUSTMENTS IF NEEDED.

Chapter 5

ORIENTATION, TRAINING AND SUPERVISION

ORIENTATION   Volunteers often need training in order to perform their agency-related jobs properly. Well designed training aims to improve the volunteer's ability to perform the specific tasks required for her or his job assignment. Volunteers may need training in answering the telephone, in decision-making processes, in counseling, in door-to-door canvassing and similar tasks. But, there is also a need for orientation to the ways in which a complex human service organization works and to the larger system of which it is a part, and to your agency's mission, its underlying values and the norms that govern staff behavior. Information about the agency's structure and its formal rules and regulations may be provided informally or in standardized presentations.

Typically, a volunteer orientation program will include the following:

- an overview of the agency, including staff organization (both paid and unpaid) and funding sources;

- the range of services offered (by whom and to whom), and how the agency fits into the larger community;

- a description of the tasks volunteers are expected to perform and what the agency will provide volunteers in return;

- how volunteers will be supervised, by whom, and with what criteria their performance will be evaluated; and

– an introduction to other staff with whom volunteers will be working.

It is important for new volunteers to meet other people at the agency and to see themselves as important to the agency's mission. This may require arranging a social activity or a small group meeting in which more experienced volunteers and/or paid staff discuss agency operations with new volunteers and spell out the volunteers' contribution to the overall effort.

Answers to specific questions about day-to-day operations will also have to be answered. If your agency or program does not have an operations manual, you will have to provide this information in some other form, preferably in writing. It is unfair to expect volunteer workers to meet expectations that have not been articulated clearly.

Informal interactions convey some of the less than formal rules and regulations—the norms that govern behavior at your agency and that specify what volunteers may or may not do. We're referring to information shared informally about "how we do it around here."

While we are on the subject of orientation, it is just as important to provide agency staff with an orientation to the volunteer program as it is to provide volunteers with an orientation to the agency. Include all staff members who might come in contact with volunteers, including clerical and maintenance personnel.

You may want to schedule one or more sessions devoted to describing the volunteer program, the role of paid staff versus volunteers, the volunteer program's objectives, how many volunteers will be involved, their training and work schedules, and how staff members will be affected in terms of supervision and or training responsibilities. Potential tensions and misunderstandings can be avoided if your staff have prior information and are given opportunities to discuss the volunteer program among themselves. This may be particularly true for the clerical staff. Secretaries and other office workers should know that there will be new people who may use office space and equipment and who may receive phone calls.

Part of your orientation activities should include a tour of the agency and introductions of staff and volunteers. You may want to provide volunteers and staff with name tags for both orientation and training sessions to facilitate the "getting to know one another" process.

TRAINING   Training differs from orientation in that it focuses on the attitudes, knowledge, and skills required to perform specific tasks. The training of volunteers is distinguishable from the training of paid staff. Volunteers often have different investments in an agency than do paid staff. The agency does not provide their livelihood. As a rule, volunteers spend considerably less time in the agency than do paid staff. The length of service of the average volunteer is generally short. In most human service agencies it is less than a year.

In designing a training program for volunteers, then, you may not want to invest as much as in training staff that are expected to stay on the job for several years and who may be on upward bound career ladders within the agency. On the other hand, we suspect that one of the reasons that volunteer turnover may be so great is that they receive insufficient training. Without good training volunteers may not be able to do their assigned jobs well or to get the intrinsic rewards they expected.

A major consideration in training volunteers is the experience they bring to the agency. Many volunteers have had previous experiences that are relevant to their assignments. They may wish to be exempted from some or all of the training program. A rule that everyone must attend all training sessions may mean losing or boring an experienced, valuable person. On the other hand, if training is mandatory for all volunteers, the agency is assured that they will be exposed to the same information or learn the same skills. If you decide to exempt for experience, be certain to explain why or how, so that no one feels that their rights have been ignored.

FOCUS OF   In designing a volunteer training program, consider
TRAINING   what the volunteer should know and be able to do, and the attitudes or perspectives that are essential to doing the job. When the focus of the training effort is on knowledge, consider what information the volunteer needs in order to do his or her job. The types and amounts of information may differ for the board member, for the direct service volunteer,

or for those engaged in clerical work, in public relations, and in fund raising.

Referring back to the job description you designed, consider that volunteers in each category should know about:

- the agency—its mandate, philosophy, history and organizational structure;
- the agency's overall program and the program or programs to which they will relate;
- the agency's client populations, special characteristics, and the needs or problems that bring them to the agency;
- the services staff provide to clients and the administrative services that keep the agency going;
- the kinds of interactions that exist between the agency and other providers of service in the community; and
- the way decisions are made about programs and policies.

What else should volunteers know? Volunteers must be able to do what is required for their appropriate category of volunteer job. The tasks they will be asked to perform can be broken down into those related to *people,* those related to *things,* and those related to *ideas.* Can you list those tasks essential to effective job performance under each category? We've started by listing some tasks in each category on the form for Exercise 7 on page 51. See if you can complete Exercise 7 by filling in as many of the blanks as possible.

Now go back over your inventory. Check [✓] those tasks that you expect volunteers to be able to perform before they come on board. *Underline* those tasks for which you think training will be necessary. For which of these is your agency prepared to provide training? At what level? Do you have some notion of the level of proficiency your volunteers should have before and after training? For example, should a clerical volunteer be able to type fifty words per minute with three or less errors?

We indicated earlier that volunteers must hold a point of view or perspective that is compatible with the agency's. That does not mean that everyone should think alike. To the contrary, you may want diversity of points of view and ideas. But there are some perspectives that may be essential to your agency's mission and its

Exercise 7

IDENTIFY THE TASKS FOR TRAINING

CATEGORY OF VOLUNTEER	TASKS TO BE PERFORMED		
	WITH PEOPLE	WITH THINGS	WITH IDEAS
Clerical or Administrative	1. answering questions on the telephone 2. _____ 3. _____ 4. _____	1. typing 2. filing 3. _____ 4. _____	1. designing a filing system 2. _____ 3. _____ 4. _____
Direct Services	1. counseling 2. home visits 3. _____ 4. _____	1. preparing hot meals 2. _____ 3. _____ 4. _____	1. evaluating the impact of a service program 2. _____ 3. _____ 4. _____
Public Relations	1. giving talks to civic groups 2. _____ 3. _____ 4. _____	1. addressing letters 2. printing brochures 3. _____ 4. _____	1. writing news releases 2. _____ 3. _____ 4. _____
Fund Raising	1. door to door collection 2. _____ 3. _____ 4. _____	1. collecting the money 2. _____ 3. _____ 4. _____	1. designing a campaign strategy 2. _____ 3. _____ 4. _____
Policy Making and Advising	1. chairing a committee 2. _____ 3. _____ 4. _____	1. _____ 2. _____ 3. _____ 4. _____	1. recommending a new program idea 2. _____ 3. _____ 4. _____

methods of operating. These may include commitments to: clients' rights of self determination; confidentiality of information on clients; respect for differences in values and life styles. On the page provided for Exercise 8, make up an inventory of attitudes and perspectives needed for each category of volunteer job. To what extent must volunteers express similar commitments prior to joining the staff? To what extent can you insure compliance through orientation and training?

Exercise 8

**INVENTORY OF ATTITUDES OR PERSPECTIVES
VOLUNTEERS SHOULD SHARE**

CATEGORY OF VOLUNTEER: [ ] Board or committee   [ ] Clerical
                           member   [ ] PR
                          [ ] Direct services   [ ] Fund raising

ON CLIENTS: _____

_____

_____

_____

ON ACCOUNTABILITY: _____

_____

_____

_____

ON LIFE STYLES
AND PLURALISM: _____

_____

_____

_____

OTHER AREAS: _____

_____

_____

_____

_____

_____

_____

DESIGNING   Refer back to your inventories of needed knowl-
A TRAINING   edge, skill, and attitudes (Exercises 7 and 8).
PROGRAM   Think through what specific knowledge, skill or
                             attitudes you want volunteers to have at the end
of training. At what level should they be able to perform? How
much do they need to be committed to clients' rights before
starting? Will some of the paid staff's attitudes rub off once
volunteers are on the job?

Having identified the training content and specified your
training objectives, it is time to move on to the design of your
training program. You may find the inventory of instructional
approaches on page 54 suggestive.

Once you have decided on your objectives, content, and
instructional approaches, check out the availability of facilities,
teaching materials, and teaching aids. Facilities include rooms and
the set-ups possible within them. Should the training occur on the
agency premises? In a hotel or retreat facility outside of town?
Are tables necessary in addition to chairs? Do you need a platform
and a lecturer? Would small rooms, set up seminar-style, make
more sense than a large activity hall?

What kinds of equipment do you need? A public address
system? Film or slide projectors? Over-head projectors? A video
tape and feed-back system? Blackboards and bulletin boards?
What about teaching aids? Which of the following are essential:
pads and pencils; newsprint pads; marking pens and tape; flip
charts and posters? Are there training guides, books, prepackaged
audio and video tapes available that deal with the issues of concern
to you?

Finally, design an evaluation procedure that will include
feedback from the learners, agency staff, and more experienced
volunteers on the effectiveness of your training program.

ON COMPLETION   Once training is over, you may want to
OF TRAINING   award trainees a "certificate of comple-
                                tion" and have them sign a "contract" for
beginning work. A sample certificate is on page 55.

If you choose to develop a work agreement or contract, the
following information should be included:

— nature of the tasks to be performed;

INVENTORY OF INSTRUCTIONAL APPROACHES

1. PRESENTATIONS: good for conveying uniform information and clarifying issues to large numbers of people in a relatively short period of time. Can be inspiring and tone setting, but require skilled presentors.

   TYPES: a. *Lectures* and mini-lectures (under 30 minutes), generally by a subject matter expert.

   b. *Interviews*—experts are interviewed by a moderator or by the audience (less formal than the lecture).

   c. *Panels*—more than one person presents a particular aspect of the topic or reacts to a lecturer's presentation.

   d. *Demonstrations*—experienced persons show the less experienced how something is done (may be followed by audience participation

   e. *Films, slides, and video tapes* may substitute for or compliment lectures, panels, and demonstrations.

2. PROBLEM SOLVING METHODS: good for putting learners into situations similar to those they may find on-the-job, leading to skill and attitude development.

   TYPES: a. *Case studies*—a problem is presented and only a part of the solution may follow. The solution is completed by trainees with instructor or group feedback.

   b. *In-basket techniques*—a problem is dropped into the trainee's "in-basket" and he or she must put the solution in an "out-basket"

   c. *Brainstorming and idea-inventorying*—all participants are asked to contribute ideas for the group to discuss.

   d. *Force field analysis or nominal group methods*—participants follow structured problem or issue clarification procedures and move progressively to collective problem solving.

3. PRACTICE SKILL DEVELOPMENT: good for learning how tasks are performed.

   TYPES: a. *Role play and psycho drama*—participants act out a work situation with guidance from an instructor and feedback from fellow learners; may be supplemented by use of video tape playback equipment.

   b. *Coaching, supervised field practice and directed internships*—learners practice on-the-job under the guidance of a more experienced volunteer or paid staff member.

   c. *Field trips and observations*—observe agency practice and may find problems that need to be addressed.

   d. *Sensitivity training*—participants learn about their own attitudes and motivations and develop skill in communicating with others.

SAMPLE TRAINING CERTIFICATE

CERTIFICATE OF COMPLETION

This is to certify that ___(volunteer's name)___ has completed a program of volunteer training on _____, 19____. Provided under the auspices of _____(agency name)_____

_____,

the training program was designed to prepare trainees for the following volunteer task: _____

_____

_____

Agency Seal	signed _____ (training director)
	_____ (date)

- number of days a month or hours per week volunteer is expected to work;
- the department or subunit to which the volunteer will be assigned;
- the supervisor and nature of supervision to be expected;
- the kind of work evaluation procedures to be used and responsibilities of both the supervisor and the volunteer in the evaluation process; and
- the duration of this contract.

Be sure to refer back to the job description you designed in Chapter 4.

Before discussing supervision and management of volunteer programs, we want to leave you with one more suggestion. You don't have to reinvent the wheel. And it is not always necessary to design and conduct a training program on your own. Consider joint volunteer training with other agencies. It is not uncommon, for example, for several mental health agencies to conduct orientation and training sessions for new board members jointly. Health and welfare councils and local volunteer bureaus often initiate training programs for volunteers performing direct service jobs from many agencies. Universities and community colleges also do volunteer training through their continuing and adult education programs.

SUPERVISING   When volunteers are fully integrated into a
THE VOLUNTEER   work unit composed primarily of paid
OR VOLUNTEER   staff, the supervisor is generally the unit
PROGRAM   supervisor or another paid worker whose
efforts are extended by the volunteer. Some paid workers find it difficult to supervise volunteers. This is especially true when a volunteer's assignment is ambiguous and when little thought has been given to identifying the units of work to be performed. Difficulties are compounded when a volunteer has been improperly oriented to the agency or poorly trained for the work expected of him or her. Paid staff may also need training for the supervision of volunteers.

Additional tensions may arise when volunteers are assigned to a paid worker for on-the-job supervision, but also receive guidance from an agency-wide coordinator whose instructions may differ from those given in the work unit. This problem can be reduced if there is clear and frequent communication between the coordinator and the work unit supervisors. If tensions arise, a meeting between the volunteer in question, the supervisor, and the volunteer coordinator can help to clarify areas of ambiguity. If volunteers occupy separate work units from staff, this type of tension is less likely. Assignments to integrated or separate work units, however, should primarily be a function of the nature of the tasks to be performed rather than an arrangement you think will be less tension-producing.

Whatever the arrangement, a number of aspects of supervision should be kept foremost in mind. Supervision can either be task-oriented, developmentally oriented, or both. Task-oriented supervision focuses on getting the job done. The supervisor may instruct (teach) or direct (indicate what is to be done and how). Developmentally oriented supervision focuses on the volunteer's improvement in skill and ability. Both orientations are needed if the volunteer is to be satisfied that he or she is doing what is required at an acceptable level while growing on the job. Supervision can take place in a one-to-one interview between the supervisor and the volunteer, in a group session in which the supervisor conducts individual supervision in a group setting so that workers with similar problems can benefit from the information exchanged, or in a collegium where the supervisor serves as a facilitator but those involved in the group session problem-solve together. Combinations of all three are possible.

In recent years, volunteer coordinators have found that supervision is most effective when the volunteer worker is fully involved in deciding what the content of the supervisory session is to be, in setting work objectives, in deciding how the work is to be performed, and in evaluating his or her own performance.

COORDINATION, MANAGEMENT AND RECORD KEEPING Some supervisors may be responsible for supervising or managing the work of many volunteers and of other supervisors. Theirs is a coordinating and managing function. Coordination is needed to avoid duplication of effort and to make certain that gaps in service are kept to a minimum. The person responsible for coordination should also check the flow of work to volunteers and paid staff to make sure that it is continuous (e.g., that case finding is not rendered ineffective because there is no one available for diagnosis and referral, or that effective preparation of mental patients to re-enter the community is not hampered by the unavailability of volunteer home help). Coordination of volunteer efforts should be incorporated in the overall managerial functions of the agency.

It is very important to maintain records on volunteer activities. This function should be assigned to either a volunteer coordinator, an experienced volunteer, or some other agency staff member. Clear records are important for evaluating your program and for helping you make decisions about the future. Records are also important to volunteers' documentation of their service and their progress.

Volunteers should have files for their application forms, job descriptions, supervision reports and other evaluative material, hours of service, and similar data. Obviously, records cannot be maintained forever. Decide on a time period for retaining them (e.g., until two years after active service), and inform volunteers

that their records will be kept for that period of time. You may
then summarize the data in the file onto a single card or page for a
permanent record. Tell the volunteer you are doing this. Everyone
has a right to know that a file is being kept and what that file
contains.

Chapter 6

WORKING WITH VOLUNTEERS AS MEMBERS OF BOARDS, TASK FORCES, AND COMMITTEES

When volunteers are members of boards, task forces, and related committees, adjustments must be made in some of the approaches to recruitment, screening, and training discussed in the previous chapters. These volunteers are engaged in policy making, in planning, and in advising activities. They may be appointed or elected to their positions.

ELECTIONS AND Boards tend to use election procedures. If
APPOINTMENTS your agency is a membership organization
such as a community center, the prospective board member may be elected by the membership-at-large or by subgroups within the organization whose interests they are to represent. In other cases, new board members may be elected by the persons currently on the board. Whether your organization has a representative board or a self-perpetuating board, the persons elected will probably have been screened and recommended by a nominating committee. The committee may be helped by paid staff to identify qualified or interested prospects.

Not all boards use election procedures, however. Appointed boards consist of persons selected by authoritative persons or groups. A county-wide alcohol services board, for example, may be composed of an equal number of persons appointed by the city council and by the county board of supervisors. A crisis center's board may be composed of representatives of several social agencies, each of whom appoint one staff member each year. Some boards are partly elected and partly appointed. A council on aging may include appointed representatives of service agencies, an equal number of persons nominated and elected by the board itself, and other members who are elected by senior citizens' groups.

In seeking prospective board members, the nominating committee may find useful some of the suggestions given for selection, recruitment, and screening of volunteers in Chapters 3, 4 and 5. It is generally a good idea to:

- check out the prospective board member's interests, qualifications and experience;
- give the prospect an idea of what will be expected or demanded of him or her;
- explain the functions of the agency and describe its major program activities or services and
- be attentive to cues and unasked questions that will help determine whether the prospect should be nominated, and which, when answered, will help the prospect choose whether or not to allow his or her name to be submitted.

BOARDS   We've used several terms thus far without defining them. A "board" of directors is generally elected or appointed to set policy for the organization, review and adopt budgets, review major programs, establish job classifications, and hire and fire the organization's chief executives and sometimes other personnel as well.

Boards usually have a set of by-laws (or agreed upon rules) under which they function. These specify procedures for nomination and election of members; amendment processes; setting goals and objectives; standing committees; establishing rules for meetings; and designation of officers and their functions.

TASK FORCES   A "task force" is generally appointed by a board of an organization or some other authoritative group or person. It may be composed exclusively of volunteers or of both paid staff and volunteers. Selection is often based on the knowledge and expertise of those selected or their strong interests and commitments to the issues around which the task force is convened. Task forces are expected to go out of business when they have completed their assigned tasks. Tasks generally include finding out the facts of a situation, solving a problem, designing a plan, or recommending a policy.

COMMITTEES   Committees may be permanent or ad hoc in nature. Boards generally have standing committees that perform specific board functions or make recommendations to the board on issues related to its functions (policy making, setting budgets, recommending job classifications and appointments, and the like.) Boards may also create special purpose ad hoc committees that function somewhat like task forces. An agency or service program's "advisory committee" presents a somewhat different case.

The advisory committee or group seldom possesses the well defined functions of policy boards and their committees. Nor does it command the same degree of authority. It may influence decisions, but not make policy. Yet, the distinctions between advising and deciding are not always clear. Lack of clarity about an advisory committee's status and authority can cause both resentment and frustration for its members and those who work with the committee. For this reason the selection process and subsequent orientation of members is vital.

OTHER   In addition to the stated functions of the board,
RESPON-   task force or committee, its members are often
SIBILITIES   expected to assume one or more of the following responsibilities:

- fostering two-way communication between the agency and a service program within it, and between the members or the organization's constituencies;

- confering legitimacy on the agency or its service programs;

- providing information on attitudes, needs or opinions of specific populations such as the agency's clients or members of various ethnic populations;

- serving as a sounding board for preliminary ideas expressed by the board or paid staff;

- acting as a buffer against attacks and criticism from external sources; or

- doing public relations, educating outside groups, or engaging in political and advocacy activities on behalf of the agency and the clients it serves.

SAMPLE
CHECK LIST OF ORGANIZATIONS
FROM WHICH TO SEEK ADVISORY COUNCIL MEMBERS
FOR AN AREA AGENCY ON AGING

Type of Member	Where to Find Them
Consumers of Services	Local senior citizen clubs, councils and associations, nutrition programs (Title VII), senior housing programs.
Associations of Older Persons	Local affiliates of the National Council of Senior Citizens, American Association of Retired Persons, Gerontological Society, National Retired Teachers Association.
Minority Groups	Ethnic and racial social clubs, National Association for the Advancement of Colored People, LASED, American Indian Movement.
Civic Groups and Fraternal Organizations	Junior League, League of Women Voters, Council of Jewish Women, Order of Eagles, Lions Club, Knights of Columbus, Rotary.
Business and Labor	Chamber of Commerce, Downtown Merchants Association, AFL-CIO Council, Board of Realtors.
Professional Groups	Bar and medical associations, societies of teachers, social workers, ministers, accountants.
Education Groups	School officials, Retired Senior Volunteer Programs, Community Colleges, Adult Education programs, libraries, boards of education.
Government Groups	Agencies which serve older people: Transportation Authority, Social Security Administration, Health Planning Organizations.
Service Organizations	Social Service agencies, Health and Mental Health Agencies, e.g., United Community Services, Visiting Nurses.
Information	Press, city and neighborhood papers, radio and television, Cable TV.

The composition of the board, task force or committee should be determined by its functions. Sometimes it makes sense for the group to be cohesive and composed of like-minded persons or of those who have similar interests, backgrounds and constituencies. At other times, a broader or a more diverse composition is desired. Persons with different or competing interests may be selected or elected.

SOURCE OF   Depending on your objectives, you may want
MEMBERSHIP   to look to a variety of sources for board, task
                            force or committee members. The checklist on page 62 was developed for recruiting advisory council members of an area agency on aging; this is an organization responsible for planning and coordinating services for older people at the local level. Look it over, then MAKE UP A CHECK LIST FOR A BOARD OR COMMITTEE IN YOUR OWN AGENCY. Then go on to Exercise 9.

Exercise 9

SPECIFYING THE WORK OF BOARDS, TASK FORCES AND COMMITTEES

It is not enough to know where to look. You'll also need to have an idea of what or whom to look for. Go back over the exercises you completed earlier. You'll recall that in a follow-up to Exercise 1, you developed a balance sheet of pros and cons of involving volunteers on boards and committees. With reference to the group you've just made a check list for, is this earlier balance sheet accurate? How might you modify it?

Would you design a recruitment handout for board and committee members similar to the one on page 36? If so, design one. To whom would you distribute it?

Can you do a job analysis for each member of the group? Do so.

Using the form for Exercise 3 as a guide, design a job description for committee, task force, or board members.

ORIENTATION   Much of the discussion in Chapter 5 applies to
AND TRAINING   orientation and training of board and com-
                       mittee members. Board and committee mem-
bers need orientation to the agency, to their roles, and to the
specific tasks assigned them. But paid staff are in a different
relationship to these volunteers. Rather than supervising them,
paid staff may be in co-equal relationships, or may be expected
only to provide technical assistance. Frequently, they are responsible to the board or committee.

For these reasons, orientation and briefings for newcomers are
often conducted by more experienced board and committee
members. Paid staff may conduct some of the sessions and do the
administrative work that goes into these briefings, but much of the
orientation may be done by fellow volunteers.

Formal training, if it is to occur, generally takes place across
organizational lines or program lines within an agency. Thus, a
single training session for board members of several rehabilitation
agencies may take place centrally. Chairpersons of different task
forces within an agency may go through a common orientation
program.

Consider including some board or committee members in
training sessions for paid and volunteer staff. Board members
often complain of inadequate board-staff relationships. This may
be one way of improving these relationships. Consider also
coordinating orientation and training with other agencies. Does it
make sense to bring together new members of all the community
mental health centers in a metropolitan area? Under whose
auspices should the training take place: a metropolitan area task
force of experienced board members; the district-wide mental
health planning board; the State Department of Mental Health; the
community services division of the local junior college; or the
United Way agency?

What are the advantages of joint training and orientation? The
disadvantages? Make yourself a list of the pros and cons. With
whom else would you have to consult on these pros and cons?

Chapter 7

THE VOLUNTEER AS ADVOCATE FOR THE AGENCY AND THE CLIENT

Advocacy is an often used, somewhat misunderstood word. Having been borrowed from the legal profession, the term has been redefined as applied to social welfare and the human services. Legal advocates get their mandate directly from the client whose legal rights they represent, whatever the right or wrong of a case. The legal advocate need not have a personal commitment to those whose interests are represented.

Not so for the human services advocate. He or she often has a personal and professional stake in redressing a wrong, or in representing the interests of a particular population in need. Volunteers can be strong advocates for your agency in the community at large and for the interests of clients and client populations within both the community and the agency.

ADVOCATING FOR THE AGENCY When board members, direct service volunteers, or others interpret the mission of the agency, they often act as passionate proponents of its programs and services. The volunteer may try to generate public support for the agency among influentials in the community or interpret the agency's services to service groups such as the Rotary Club, the Kiwanis, and others. He or she may publicize the agency's programs informally among friends or more formally with representatives of the news media.

Often, the volunteer interprets the agency's programs to specific populations. Volunteers from RSVP (Retired Senior Volunteer Program) may reach out to older persons, informing them about the programs of golden age clubs or about the counseling services available at the family agency. Volunteers for an adoption agency may go beyond interpretation of the agency's services to recruiting potential adoptive families for special needs children. They often correct misconceptions about the services provided by the agency and attempt to generate interest and support for them.

The use of volunteers as advocates for the agency is, unfortunately, too often ad hoc and unplanned. If your agency has a coordinator or supervisor for the volunteer program, that person should support the volunteers' natural desire to advocate for the agency. The same kind of handouts and other materials that go into a volunteer recruitment effort might be useful for "agency interpretation". What can you do in your agency to support the volunteers' efforts? Exercise 10 may help you think through a more systematic approach to working with your volunteers as advocates.

ADVOCATING   Volunteers are often strong advocates for
FOR THE   clients and clients' rights. They may feel that
CLIENT   your agency is not operating in accordance
                 with its stated objectives or in conformance
with its public mandate and the law. They may feel that some services are inappropriate or ill conceived and that the reasons for this lie in the ignorance, ill will, or inappropriate attitudes of some staff.

Frequently, the volunteer is quite correct. He or she may be in a good position to see things from the clients' point of view and to reflect that point of view to paid staff. The volunteer may have closer personal contacts with clients and may be less bound by long standing commitments to agency policy or procedures. Although volunteers are also subject to their own problems of tunnel vision, their points of view deserve careful consideration.

In almost every human service setting, some clients are deprived of access to needed services. The volunteer may press hard to see that these persons get a bigger share or distribution of the services available. When resources are limited, redistribution may result in

Exercise 10
VOLUNTEER ADVOCACY FOR THE AGENCY

	Suggestions	
1. List things that volunteers could do to advocate for the agency or its programs.	Think of a specific program or programs and what volunteer advocates might do.	
2. Which volunteers or categories of volunteers should do them?	Think of specific volunteers as categories such as board and committee members, direct services volunteers, etc.	
3. How could these efforts be coordinated with other efforts of paid staff?	Think of other activities going on and those that should be started.	
4. Who should coordinate volunteer efforts?	The staff with whom volunteers currently interact? The extension director? The volunteer coordinator?	
5. What kinds of supportive materials could the agency provide?	Are there some currently available or do new materials have to be developed? By whom?	

You may wish to duplicate this exercise and use several forms for different tasks and categories of volunteers.

a smaller distribution of services to other populations. In other situations, the issue may not be a scarcity or maldistribution of services, but ineffective linkage mechanisms between clients and provider. Potential clients may not know about the agency's services. Agency staff may use language and helping approaches that alienate potential clients. Volunteers can advocate for both by helping establish better communication procedures and more effective outreach, intake, or referral mechanisms.

Client advocacy is not always comfortable either for the volunteer or for the paid staff. The latter may feel defensive when shortcomings are pointed out. The volunteer may find him or herself in a rather difficult position when his or her perceptions of what needs doing are in conflict with the agency's normal way of doing things.

This is a natural phenomenon and should be expected wherever an extensive volunteer program is developed. It is often planned for in the recruitment and training of board or committee members. These persons are often selected because they are expected to advocate for the client. Why should this not be a normal expectation for direct service and other volunteers?

In Exercise 11, we ask you to think through some of the issues implied in client advocacy that your agency is currently facing.

Exercise 11
CLIENT ADVOCACY

1. Are volunteers performing any client advocacy activities at your agency now? List several. You may find it useful to list them under each category of volunteers at the agency.

2. Of the activities identified, which do you think are appropriate; which are inappropriate? Why? Which need integrating? Which should be keyed down?

3. What additional client advocacy activities should be promoted?

4. Do formal channels exist through which client volunteers can perform client advocacy? Or, is each incident handled in an ad hoc manner, case by case?

5. How could the agency improve or expand the client advocacy activities of its volunteers?

Chapter 8

EVALUATING VOLUNTEERS AND
THE VOLUNTEER PROGRAM

Evaluation is essential to maintaining a high quality volunteer program. It can provide you with ways of measuring how your program is doing, both on an individual and programmatic level. On the individual level, evaluation is often a component of supervision. It includes regularly scheduled feedback between the volunteer and the relevant paid staff member. It focuses on the performance of the individual volunteer, his or her areas of strength, and the areas that need improvement as perceived by the volunteer, the supervisor, and other staff.

At the programmatic level, evaluation focuses on the effectiveness and efficiency of the volunteer program. Effectiveness measures how close the program comes to meeting its stated objectives. Efficiency measures the costs associated with the program in relation to its benefits.

INDIVIDUAL   In many agencies, state or national regulations
EVALUATION   require that volunteers operate under the
                      supervision of an agency director or his or her
appointee. If supervision and evaluation are to be meaningful, volunteers must know to whom they are responsible and what criteria are being used to measure their performance. Both the supervisor and the volunteer should have clear standards of performance upon which to base evaluation. These should be

consistent with the original job description used to employ the individual and the units of work associated with that description. Some agencies use paid staff to supervise and evaluate volunteers. Others employ older, more experienced volunteers to supervise newer ones. Experienced volunteers may be most familiar with the job, and may be able to provide real insight into the position of being a volunteer in the agency. Whomever is chosen to supervise, it is important that these persons understand their roles and make clear the basis on which evaluation is being conducted.

If the volunteers in your agency provide direct services to clients, it is generally a good idea to use their completed client contact forms or written logs of their interactions with clients or client groups. These records may be useful to the supervisor who can then take responsibility for follow-up both with clients and the volunteers. Assuming safeguards to assure confidentiality for both the agency's clients and the volunteers, these documents may also be helpful to review committees, composed of paid staff and experienced volunteers, who may be responsible for evaluating the overall volunteer program.

It is important to provide periodic and structured opportunities for feedback between volunteers and paid staff, between volunteers and the volunteer coordinator or agency administrator, and between paid staff and the volunteer coordinator or administrator. Ways to structure feedback include:

- conferences, either formal or informal, regularly scheduled between supervisors and volunteers to discuss written forms and job-specific issues;

- written evaluation forms completed by supervisors and shared with volunteers. These should discuss individual strengths and areas and methods for improvement, including specific examples of both "good" and "bad" job performances; and

- written forms completed by volunteers and made available to supervisors which include evaluation of self, supervision, program and specific job, and suggestions for change or improvement.

Volunteers, like all staff members, should receive both positive and negative feedback. A balance of the two generally helps people develop a realistic image of their performance. In addition, volunteers can provide useful feedback to paid staff including the volunteer coordinator, if your agency has one. Every agency needs an established, systematic way to deal with volunteers who are not performing their jobs competently. Dismissal is one option. Volunteers and paid staff must be aware of who has the authority to dismiss a volunteer, under what circumstances, and using which procedures. Procedures for appeal should also be formalized and made known to all concerned.

It is often preferable to retrain volunteers who are not performing their jobs adequately, particularly if the individual is highly motivated, and if training is an appropriate response to the problem. At other times, poor performance is related to an inappropriate matching of the volunteer to the assignment. One volunteer may be more suited to PR work than to direct service; another would be quite capable of driving handicapped clients to health services, but totally inept at providing counseling services. Units of work may be improperly designed or volunteers inappropriately assigned to the wrong work units. In either case, poor performance of the volunteer may suggest problems with the program itself.

PROGRAM   Evaluating the program is a more complex
EVALUATION   process than evaluating the individual volunteer. Program evaluation can be on-going or periodic. On-going evaluation is sometimes referred to as monitoring. It requires gathering data on all aspects of a program on a regular basis and using that information to make necessary adjustments. For example, recruitment efforts may not be bringing in the necessary number of volunteers. A new recruitment technique can be introduced and its effectiveness can be measured in terms of whether or not it made a difference. Efficiency can be measured by determining whether or not the costs were justified by the results. Your turn-over rate may be increasing, which is costly to the agency in terms of training and of the effectiveness of a particular service your agency is trying to render. You may discover that there were not enough incentives, that tasks were too stressful, and that the costs volunteers had to incur in out-of-pocket expenses were too high.

Changes can be introduced to alleviate the problem identified. The types of changes implied by the information gathered in evaluation should be made with the participation of those who designed the program and involve other appropriate staff and volunteers. Then, you must evaluate again to see if the changes you've introduced make a difference.

In contrast to on-going evaluation, periodic evaluation occurs at specified times. It may be an annual or semi-annual process. Or, it may take place at the end of a project period. Periodic program evaluation is used to take stock and to determine what should happen next.

Whether on-going or periodic, program evaluation is concerned with the following questions:

- Is the program meeting its objectives? To what extent? Were the initial objectives appropriate or should they be reexamined with a view towards modification or reaffirmation?

- If the program does not meet agreed upon objectives or if the objectives are no longer appropriate, should the volunteer program be phased out?

- Assuming agreement on objectives, can the volunteer program be improved? Can it be adjusted to changing conditions such as pressures to serve new client populations, new sources of income, changes in the methods of service delivery, new relationships to other service providers?

- To what extent can evaluation help the volunteer program become more effective or efficient?

- Should it be expanded?

- How can the evaluation process accommodate the need of the agency to be accountable to its funders, to the public at large, and to its clients or board of directors?

The more comprehensive your overall evaluation, the more questions you will be able to answer. How comprehensive you want your evaluation design to be depends on what you really need to know, the resources you want to spend on getting the answers, the expertise available to you, and the demands for evaluation from internal and external sources.

Consider using volunteers in evaluation tasks. One mental health center assigned a knowledgeable volunteer to evaluate the efficiency of the volunteer program. She gathered information on costs associated with supervision, training, and recruitment and compared those costs to the cost to the agency of using paid rather than volunteer staff to perform, in this case, telephone counseling. The results of the study were presented to the agency's board during a budget allocation meeting. More funds were allocated to recruitment and training categories as a result of the study.

Client feedback can be an important component of an evaluation design. Think about designing a questionnaire to find out client responses to services rendered by volunteers, particularly those providing direct service. If your questionnaire is objective, short, and confidential, you may be able to get some very useful information in terms of how volunteers are perceived by clients, areas in which better training or selection procedures might be introduced, and similar information.

One program did a client survey at the completion of a project run by volunteers. The results indicated that clients, overall, felt that the volunteers were competent and performed their tasks well, except in the initial interview. A majority of the client responses indicated that the volunteers appeared anxious and defensive during that first contact. This information was used to design future training programs with more emphasis on initial interviewing skills. It is likely that this problem would have been noticed by individual supervisors, but it probably would not have been translated as quickly into a training need for the program.

Evaluation will not always bring in such positive results. You may find that costs are too high or that the program is not meeting certain important objectives. But knowing is better than not knowing. If you don't know what's wrong, you cannot make necessary changes.

At this point, we suggest that you review each of the preceding chapters as well as the procedures used to evaluate other aspects of your agency's program. Do these suggest what would be evaluated and how? Decide what it is you want to know. Do you want to know how many clients are seen by each direct service volunteer? How much does it cost in paid staff time to work with volunteers in fund-raising activities and how much income is generated from these activities? Are you more interested in focusing on the recruitment and training aspects of your volunteer program? On the relationships between paid and volunteer staff?

Once you have decided what it is you want to know, think

through a similar set of questions from the point of view of the volunteer, the agency's board, and the agency's funding source. Different groups may expect different answers to the same questions or may want different questions answered. Which ones do you wish to answer? Which ones must you answer?

Consider getting help from persons either within your organization or outside who have expertise in program evaluation. Put together a team of people including an expert in evaluation, your volunteer coordinator, and appropriate paid and volunteer staff. Do it early in your planning.

Evaluation designs that are built into a program right from the start are not only more likely to be on target but also may help you be more explicit about your program's objectives and the means you will use to reach them.

APPENDIX A

APPENDIX A

BIBLIOGRAPHY

Ash, Philip (ed.)
Volunteers for Mental Health.
New York: MSS Information Corp., 1973

A book of readings prepared for college psychology courses. It is primarily focused on aspects of using students as volunteers in mental health settings and presents some interesting case studies of volunteer programs as well as reviews of research studies on the use of volunteers.

Cull, John G. and Richard E. Hardy (eds.)
Volunteerism: An Emerging Profession.
Springfield, Illinois: Charles C Thomas, 1974.

Covers recruitment, supervision, research and communication needs in voluntary action, and community organization planning.

Hardy, Richard E. and John C. Cull (eds.).
Applied Volunteerism in Community Development.
Springfield, Illinois: Charles C Thomas, 1973.

Provides case studies of different kinds of volunteer programs and various types of volunteers. Has an informative section describing federal volunteer programs.

Hartogs, Nelly and Joseph Weber.
Boards of Directors: A Study of Current Practices in Board Management and Operations in Voluntary Hospital, Health and Welfare Organizations.
New York: Oceana Publications, Inc., 1974.

Interesting findings for agency administrators, board members and staff.

Kolton, Marilyn, Louis Dwarshius, Michael Gorodezky and Anne Dosher.
Innovative Approaches to Youth Services.
Madison, Wisconsin: STASH Press, 1973.

Based on information gathered during three conferences held in 1971 and 1972 on innovative community drug programs for youth. Two chapters of notes on "Volunteers" and "Training" are particularly useful.

Lauffer, Armand
Doing Continuing Education and Staff Development.
New York: McGraw Hill Books, 1978.

In a basic text on the design of staff development programs, the author tells how to design one, where to locate it, how to finance it, and similar information.

Lauffer, Armand et. al.
Understanding Your Social Agency.
Beverly Hills, California: Sage Publications, Inc., 1977.

Seven perspectives on organizations are described. Each is useful in dealing with service delivery problems or with staff relationships. This volume is an important adjunct to Chapters 1 and 2.

Loeser, Herta.
Women, Work and Volunteering.
Boston: Beacon Press, 1974.

Primarily aimed at women (and men) who are contemplating volunteerism, either as a temporary or permanent commitment. Deals with many of the motivations which influence volunteering, and provides interesting case illustrations of different types of volunteer positions. Has useful appendices and an extensive bibliography.

Routh, Thomas A.
The Volunteer and Community Agencies.
Springfield, Illinois: Charles C Thomas, 1972.

Aimed at demonstrating the importance of formal training, recruitment and supervision of volunteers. Explores, within that context, the relationship between clients, the agency, staff and volunteers.

Schindler-Rainman, Eva and Ronald Lippitt.
The Volunteer Community: Creative Use of Human Resources.
Washington, D.C.: National Training Laboratory for Applied Behavioral Science, 1971.

One of the best books around on the phenomenon of volunteerism, it examines both the present and future potentials for volunteer activity. Chapters 4-7 are most useful.

Soroker, Gerald S.
Fund Raising for Philanthropy.
Pittsburgh: Pittsburgh Jewish Publication and Education Foundation, 1974.

A detailed analysis of all aspects of fund raising. This book discusses the role of the volunteer in fund raising and how this role can be executed for successful fund-raising campaigns.

Stenzel, Anne K. and Helen M. Feeney.
Volunteer Training and Development: A Manual for Community Groups.
New York: Seabury Press, 1968.

Each of the chapters includes sample forms, charts and "how to" sections. The book provides useful step-by-step procedures for establishing, developing and maintaining a volunteer program.

Trecker, Harleigh B.
Citizen Boards at Work.
New York: Association Press, 1970.

Covers many types of citizen boards, including the roles of policy boards, administrative boards, advisory commissions and committees working in community service environments; and includes both research findings, theoretical discussions, reviews of literature in these areas, and practical suggestions for improving board functioning.

You might also want to subscribe to *Volunteer Administration*, a Quaty Publication.

APPENDIX B

APPENDIX B

ADDITIONAL SOURCES OF INFORMATION

ACTION
806 Connecticut Avenue
Washington, D.C. 20625

This is a recently created federal umbrella agency which administers such volunteer programs as Foster Grandparents, Retired Senior Volunteer Program (RSVP), Active Core of Executives (ACE), Service Core of Retired Executives (SCORE), the Peace Corps, Vista, and the National Student Volunteer Program. Limited grants are available for implementing some of the programs in local agencies, as well as some program development consultation.

American Association of Volunteer Services Coordinators
18 South Michigan Avenue, Suite 602
Chicago, Illinois 60603

Open to paid coordinators of volunteer programs, this association is primarily concerned with promoting volunteer administration as a profession, including the development of standards and higher education training.

American National Red Cross
17th and D Streets, NW
Washington, D.C. 20006

Both administrative and program guidance.

American Society of Directors of Voluntary Services of the American Hospital Association
840 North Lake Shore Drive
Chicago, Illinois 60611

Open to those with primary responsibility for volunteer programs within health care settings.

Association of Junior Leagues of America
    825 Third Avenue
    New York, New York 10022

Association of Volunteer Bureaus
    P.O. Box 125
    801 North Fairfax Street
    Alexandria, Virginia 22314

    Provides consultation to agencies and community groups on volunteerism and recruits; refers individual volunteers.

Center for a Voluntary Society
    1785 Massachusetts Avenue
    Washington, D.C. 20036

    Conducts research on volunteerism, sponsors workshops and conferences on pertinent volunteer issues, and provides consultation services.

Girl Scouts of the U.S.A.
    830 Third Avenue
    New York, New York 10022

    Excellent "recruitment" and "training" materials.

National Center for Voluntary Action
    1785 Massachusetts Avenue, N.W.
    Washington, D.C. 20036

    A clearinghouse on all aspects of volunteer service programming, the Center has developed a network of local voluntary action centers.

National Council on the Aging, Inc.
    1828 L Street, N.W., Suite 504
    Washington, D.C. 20036

National Council of Jewish Women
    1 West 47th Street
    New York, New York 10036

    Excellent program materials.

National Information Center on Volunteerism, Inc.
    1221 University Avenue
    Boulder, Colorado 80302

    Primarily concerned with but not restricted to volunteer activities related to courts and other criminal justice programs. This center publishes a newsletter and conducts training programs.

National Institute of Mental Health
   5600 Fishers Lane
   Rockville, Maryland
   A collection of studies and project reports.

National School Volunteer Program
   Los Angeles City Public Schools
   450 North Grand Avenue
   Los Angeles, California
   Provides information, publishes a newsletter and conducts an annual conference.

The Source Collective
   P.O. Box 21066
   Washington, D.C. 20009
   Provides information on change-oriented voluntary groups and resources. Has published material on many voluntary organizations, books, and films.

United Way of America
   345 East 46th Street
   New York, New York 10017
   Information on voluntary participation.

Veterans Administration—UAVS Program
   810 Vermont Avenue, N.W.
   Washington, D.C.
   Excellent materials on working with organizations and special projects.

Volunteer Insurance Service Organization
   5513 Connecticut Avenue, N.W.
   Washington, D.C. 20015
   A non-profit organization which researches available and feasible insurance relating to volunteers. Compiles underwriting information, maintains a central insurance library, furnishes information to agency members, and designs insurance covering volunteers.

Volunteers in Probation
   A Division of the National Council on Crime and Delinquency
   200 Washington Square Plaza
   Royal Oak, Michigan 48067
   Assists in developing volunteer programs in courts and correctional institutions. Provides speakers, consultants, workshops, and written and visual material on volunteer programs in the courts.

Other Publications of Interest in the Sage-University of Michigan Handbooks for the Human Services:

Bertcher, Harvey J. and Frank F. Maple.
   Creating Groups (Sage Human Services Guides, Volume 2). Beverly Hills, California: Sage Publications, Inc., 1977.

Lauffer, Armand et. al.
   Grantsmanship (Sage Human Services Guides, Volume 1). Beverly Hills, California: Sage Publications, Inc., 1977.

_____.
   Understanding Your Social Agency (Sage Human Services Guides, Volume 3). Beverly Hills, California: Sage Publications, Inc. 1977.

_____.
   Volunteers (Sage Human Services Guides, Volume 5). Beverly Hills, California: Sage Publications, Inc., 1977.

Maple, Frank F.
   Shared Decision Making (Sage Human Services Guides, Volume 4). Beverly Hills, California: Sage Publications, Inc., 1977.

ABOUT THE AUTHORS

ARMAND LAUFFER, editor of this series, is Professor of Social Work at the University of Michigan where he has been director of the University's Continuing Education Program in the Human Services, the largest, most varied program of its kind in the country. He is serving as visiting professor at the Hebrew University of Jerusalem, Israel, during the 1977-1978 and 1978-1979 academic years.

SARAH GORODEZKY received her undergraduate degree in Social Sciences from the University of California, Berkeley and an M.A. in Continuing Education from the University of Michigan. During her affiliation with the Continuing Education Program, School of Social Work at the University of Michigan, Ms. Gorodezky planned conferences and workshops for human service personnel, including volunteers and volunteer administrators. She also has several years experience as a volunteer in community agencies. Ms. Gorodezky is currently coordinating special programs in Gerontological Services for the University of California Extension at Santa Barbara.